Brooklyn Flavored Haiku

By Kim B Miller

Some haiku were previously published in books:

My Poetry Is the Beauty Your Overlook

Poetically Inking: Just Me, My Pen & The Mic

17 Syllables of Poetic Ammo

Copyright © 2015, 2020, 2025 Kim B Miller

All rights reserved.

Kim B Miller LLC

www.kimbmiller.com

ISBN: 979-8-9928445-1-1

Dedication

I dedicate all my poetic words to Jesus. He gives me the strength to speak truth.

I'd also like to thank Butterfly Free for performing haiku at an open mic (years ago) and exposing me to this beautiful form of poetry.

Front Cover

The cover was created in Canva.

All artistic pictures and elements are in Canva's database.

The adaption of the Brooklyn Bridge was created in craiyon.com.

Back Cover

The picture of Kim was taken by Katherine Costello Photography.

This is my analysis, please do your own research.

What are 5-7-5 haiku?

Traditional haiku are Japanese poems that are only about nature.

In that form:
- Every line should have a complete thought
- Words cannot be broken up and continued on the following line
- No rhyming
- Capitalization can vary depending on who writes the poem.
- The 1st line has 5 syllables, the 2nd line has 7 syllables, and the 3rd line has 5 syllables.
- 17 syllables total (not 17 words)

What are 5-7-5 senryu?

Senryu are what many poets call nontraditional haiku. They were originally Japanese poems on human follies.

Many years ago, someone, not Kim, decided to broaden senryu to include any subject.

In that form:

- Every line does not have to be a complete thought
- Words can be broken up and continued on the following line
- Capitalization can vary depending on who writes the poem.
    - Some writers capitalize the beginning of each line even in the middle of a word
        - I personally do not like this form because it is confusing to read.

Senryu continued:

- o I believe haikuists should use capitalization and punctuation the way they would normally use it, to make it easier for a reader to understand the poem written.
  - The 1st line has 5 syllables, the 2nd line has 7 syllables, and the 3rd line has 5 syllables.
  - 17 syllables total (not 17 words)

Reciting haiku:

Even though haiku and senryu have 2 distinctive meanings, when poets recite them, they typically don't make a differentiation. Most spoken word poets call all 17 syllabled poems haiku even if they may actually be senryu.

Table Of Contents

Name	Page
Chapter 1: Inspirational Haiku	1
Chapter 2: Relationship or Not Haiku	23
Chapter 3: Let's Talk Women Haiku	43
Chapter 4: Let's Talk Men Haiku	72
Chapter 5: Heal Haiku	84
Chapter 6: Red, Black & Green Haiku	120
Chapter 7: I Said What I Said	134
Chapter 8: In Your Face Haiku	179
Chapter 9: Quieter Punch Haiku	205
Chapter 10: Whispering Facts Haiku	228
Chapter 11: Poet-factual Haiku	253

Inspirational Haiku

Someone is waiting
for you to fail and give up.
Let's keep them waiting!

It's okay to be
scared, do it anyway. Scared
people succeed too.

There is no such thing
as the right time but there is
a time you make right.

Haiku

> You focused on a setback while progress is waiting. You ain't done yet.

You focused on a setback while progress is waiting. You ain't done yet.

A mistake can be
a lesson. Don't ignore it.
Find the real message.

Haiku

> My people, stop looking for the help you want and be the help you need.

My people, stop looking for the help you want and be the help you need.

If your passion can't
pay your bills let it fill your
soul. Love what you do.

You were looking for
someone
powerful. I just
showed you your
mirror.

You were looking for someone powerful. I just showed you your mirror.

Though it ends is "s"
happiness is not plural.
All you need is you.

Don't ask permission
to be great. You did not ask
permission to fail.

They thought they broke you
but you are a glow stick. They
just exposed your light.

> Be who you are,
> not
> to impress but to inspire.
> Let your greatness drip.

Be who you are, not
to impress but to inspire.
Let your greatness drip.

Stop using excus-
es to be small and go make
reasons to be great!

Facts spoke: no one can stop you but you. There's no age-based timeline for growth.

Your peace is not conditional on anyone else. It's self-defined.

Yesterday's mistakes
don't erase today's progress.
Potential still lives.

Fear is too comfortable with you. Give her an eviction notice.

You don't need
their parachute.
You don't need
them to pilot as
you soar.

You don't need their parachute. You don't need them to pilot as you soar.

Stop erasing your achievements. Look small for who? Let their ego trip.

Don't bury you're abilities because you made a mistake. Mourn pride!

Your elevation
is just starting. Change ain't your
enemy. Free her!

Relationship Haiku

You have all of the
ingredients for love but
no real recipe.

Are you missing a pattern or a person? It's time you seeked the truth.

Haiku

You cannot have a future with someone if they won't deal with their past.

You cannot have a future with someone if they won't deal with their past.

Haiku

You're trauma bonding
with people and calling it
a relationship.

You are angry with
who stayed while romanticizing the one who left.

If you need someone
else to complete you, you'll always
be incomplete.

Your heart wouldn't mind if you stop dating your ex. Excuses don't dry tears.

Haiku

You glorify memories while blurring facts. They did not deserve you!

It's not too much work
to love you. Block that echo.
Let that lie die now.

Haiku

If you give them the key to your joy, when they leave, they can take the lock.

The love you lost was never yours to keep. You are not a human crutch!

Your love is only
puddle deep and this ocean
won't deal with puddles.

When was the last time
you loved yourself like you're trying to love your boo.

Companionship is
not a solution to pain.
Don't give love a job.

Love began to see
you were thirsty for the wrong
reasons so she left.

Haiku

You're not good at goodbyes. You just quit people before they can quit you.

You're not good at good byes. You just quit people before they can quit you.

Since zero times two
equals zero. Why are you
two still together?

Haiku

> The thought of you becoming stronger without me. (Sigh) Who's your new crutch?

The thought of you becoming stronger without me. (Sigh) Who's your new crutch?

Write a Relationship or Not Haiku

_____

_____

_____

Haiku
Let's Talk Women

He might not have a degree but that don't mean he can't educate you.

The only reason
you still have him
is because
she don't want
him back!

The only reason
you still have him is because
she don't want him back!

Strong women are not
unbreakable. We just know
you ain't the hammer.

Haiku

> You were looking for someone beautiful. I just showed you your mirror.

You were looking for someone beautiful. I just showed you your mirror.

Haiku

You can't determine
a man's worth by
the car he drives.
Who's the scrub
now?

You can't determine
a man's worth by the car he
drives. Who's the scrub now?

Haiku

Are you his queen or the head pawn? He's moving the pieces. Check your mate!

Haiku

Real truth, men are not the only ones who are not faithful. Right ladies?

Real truth, men are not the only ones who are not faithful. Right ladies?

Why shouldn't he cheat on
you, when you cheat on you.
Crumbs are all you want Sis!

Haiku

> A man isn't a shield
> to your insecurities.
> Your pain ain't his job.

A man isn't a shield
to your insecurities.
Your pain ain't his job.

Why are you
letting
someone who
carries a 6
pack, dictate your
weight?

Why are you letting someone who carries a 6 pack, dictate your weight?

Haiku

It's not too late for you to succeed. It's time you stopped blaming him though.

You ain't cute for
a (fill in the
stereotype).
You're cute
PERIOD!

You ain't cute for a
(fill in the stereotype).
You're cute PERIOD!

Women, please don't hurt
other women with the words
men use to hurt us.

Men are not our "smiling mechanics". Smile only when you feel like it.

Haiku

You can't change him! Ladies, you will never "be enough" for the wrong man.

You can't change him! Ladies, you will never "be enough" for the wrong man.

Haiku

He ain't a walking
cash register. He's a man.
Make your own money!

Haiku

He cannot lift you, not because of your weight. It is your baggage Sis.

He cannot lift you,
not because of your weight. It
is your baggage Sis.

Haiku

Ladies, if you keep
kissing frogs how
will you know
what a prince
tastes like?

Ladies, if you keep
kissing frogs how will you know
what a prince tastes like?

Haiku

You picked a clown and
got mad when he wore makeup
better than you did.

> Your makeup is your blanket 'cause pretty is more important than pain.

Your makeup is your blanket 'cause pretty is more important than pain.

Haiku

> Once you find the right king, you won't have to play chess. He won't want the pawns.

Once you find the right
king, you won't have to play chess.
He won't want the pawns.

Stop blaming men for having baggage when you have a storage unit!

Haiku

> Men fight for what they want. If you have to chase him then, he don't want you!

Men fight for what they want. If you have to chase him then, he don't want you!

Haiku

> Women, please get uncomfortable. Get in your own face! Just do it scared!

Women, please get uncomfortable. Get in your own face! Just do it scared!

Haiku

> Girls, do not let
> some boy tell you
> you're not
> powerful, like
> they would know.

Girls, do not let some boy tell you you're not powerful, like they would know.

Haiku

> Ladies, our resilience is great but our self-care needs to be greater.

Ladies, our resil-
ience is great but our self-care
needs to be greater.

Everything is not
our fault. Stop picking up oth-
er people's baggage.

Write a Let's Talk Women Haiku

_____

_____

_____

Haiku

Let's Talk Men

Haiku

> Understand that if you have to tell me you're "the man", you're not "the man".

Understand that if
you have to tell me you're "the
man", you're not "the man".

Haiku

You're worried about
the thug she's
dating when you
were her first thug
dad.

You're worried about
the thug she's dating when you
were her first thug dad.

Dear King, she's in love,
with love and you can't compete
with a fantasy.

Let yourself be loved
by the right person. Your past
is "heart blocking" you.

Sir you can't upgrade
me. I don't need upgrading.
I need a new man.

Haiku

Just stop comparing women. Flowers can grow in more than one garden.

Haiku

Slowing down your pace to get her, why? If she can't hustle, leave her there!

Slowing down your pace to get her, why? If she can't hustle, leave her there!

You're a distraction.
She's waiting for her king and
settling for you.

Haiku

You told her goodbye
but now you're looking back. Why?
Old garbage still stinks.

Haiku

She's in love with your words but your heart did not write them. Tell her who did.

She's in love with your words but your heart did not write them. Tell her who did.

In order for her
to be a gold digger, don't
you have to have gold?

Heal Haiku

Haiku

People can't validate
you out of your insecurities,
that's your job!

No one will miss me!
That's a lie! Lies talk to those
willing to listen.

Haiku

> Maybe she's the one who understands the braille his pain is written in.

Maybe she's the one who understands the braille his pain is written in.

Haiku

> Maybe he's the
> one who
> understands the
> braille her
> pain is written in.

Maybe he's the one
who understands the braille her
pain is written in.

Haiku

Stop getting used. Start creating boundaries. No revenge is needed.

Haiku

You have calendar
fillers, not soul fulfillers.
Schedule time with truth.

Haiku

How many of you
are buried in words from your
past? Let old scars heal.

Haiku

Their doubts are starting
to feel like your truth 'cause you
absorbed orphaned fear.

Their doubts are starting
to feel like your truth 'cause you
absorbed orphaned fear.

Haiku

You need to stop giving people the pen and paper to judge you with.

You need to stop giving people the pen and paper to judge you with.

Haiku

The power you give
their validation is kill-
ing you. Peace can't breathe.

Haiku

Your mental health is suffering. Everyone's needs can't supersede yours.

Your mental health is suffering. Everyone's needs can't supersede yours.

Haiku

If your pain runs deep,
why is your response so shallow? Read that again!

You cannot be an
anchor for them and swim too.
Drowning ain't a flex!

Haiku

Don't ghost the people
who give you honest feedback.
Drain the "yes" fountain.

Haiku

Some of you are blaming yourself for being cut by broken people.

You're throwing money
at pain but pain won't make change
with your excuses.

Haiku

You were not born just
to be an answer to someone's
brokenness. Live!

How are you going
to get closure on hurt or
pain, you won't open?

Haiku

> Do not let people
> use the flawed
> parts of you to
> make something
> ugly.

Do not let people
use the flawed parts of you to
make something ugly.

Cultivate a rhythm of reflection. Hope cannot breathe without you.

Cultivate a rhythm of reflection. Hope cannot breathe without you.

Self-love only grows
if you water it but you
can't use your own tears.

Haiku

Let's normalize accepting feedback and stop calling it an attack.

Let's normalize accepting feedback and stop calling it an attack.

My strength supersedes
my situation. My pain
does not speak for me.

How many times do
you have to fall before you
stop tripping yourself?

Haiku

Why don't you sit with your victories, like you sit with your failures?
Well?

Why don't you sit with your victories, like you sit with your failures? Well?

I can help you, help
you but I can't help you, if
you won't help yourself.

Haiku

If your pain runs deep
why is your response so shallow.
Read that again.

If your pain runs deep
why is your response so shallow. Read that again.

Haiku

You are not a walking mistake. You're an undiscovered miracle.

You are not a walking mistake. You're an undiscovered miracle.

Haiku

When that wave of pain comes, don't forget you can swim! Can't drown standing up.

When that wave of pain comes, don't forget you can swim! Can't drown standing up.

Haiku

> Stop cutting people off 'cause they didn't check on you when they were hurting.

Stop cutting people
off 'cause they didn't check on you
when they were hurting.

You are not a broken people repair kit! They can heal without you!

You are not a broken people repair kit! They can heal without you!

You cannot divide yourself into fractions to make someone else whole.

> Your mental health is
> not someone
> else's job. Love
> ain't free therapy.

Your mental health is
not someone else's job. Love
ain't free therapy.

Get counseling. Your
mate is not your therapist.
They are your victim!

I'm not trying to
be better than you. I'm try-
ing to be better.

Haiku
Red, Black & Green

Haiku

I'll just sit this here.
What if God treated you, like
you treat Black people?

I'll just sit this here.
What if God treated you, like
you treat Black people?

When a flower dies,
the forest cries. They don't check
the flower's hue first.

Haiku

Blacks are drunk on compliments about our articulation: tongue slurs!

Dear Black people, don't
make rules for other Black peo-
ple, signed who asked you!

Haiku

If there's no Earth to live on, will you care if your rescuers are Black?

We make everything about race because race is about everything.

Believe in Black businesses even if that means sacrificing lies.

Haiku

> We are Black butterflies, trying to get some to see that we have wings.

We are Black butter-
flies, trying to get some to
see that we have wings.

Haiku

We have the right to remain silent but our "Black hair" needs a lawyer.

You do realize
that Martin's dream was not the
speech but real change, right?

It's February,
so, it's time for Blacks to be
history again.

Haiku

Black diamond, yes Sis
that's you sparkle! That self-love
flex is different.

We throw cards, spades. Smack big jokers and talk trash. No sportsmanship, just win!

I had a dream that
Martin made
more than just one
speech. Are you
awake?

I had a dream that
Martin made more than just one
speech. Are you awake?

Haiku
I Said What I Said

You're not a friend. You're
an acquaintance used for their
mental maintenance.

Haiku

You're not a people pleaser, you're a pain avoider. Truth can see you.

You're not a people pleaser, you're a pain avoider. Truth can see you.

Haiku

You tried and failed
you cannot take
stupid and make
it a profession.

You tried and failed you cannot take stupid and make it a profession.

> Freedom does not equal free. It just means your illusionist is free.

Freedom does not equal free. It just means your illusionist is free.

Haiku

When your thirst outweighs
your fears, you'll work on your goals
but you ain't thirsty!

Temptation is just
a test to see if we are
who we say we are.

Just because they're in your nest that does not mean they want to see you fly.

Yes, I admit I

was wrong but me being wrong

does not make you right!

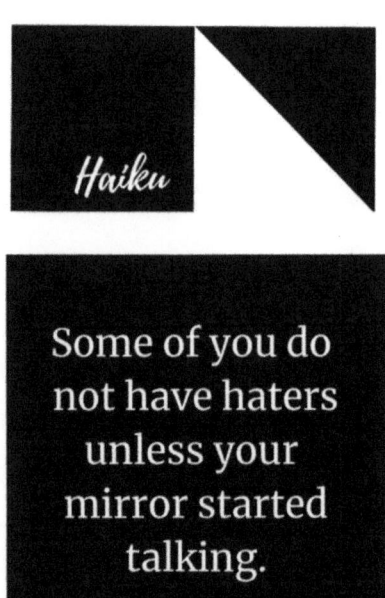

Some of you do not
have haters unless your mir-
ror started talking.

I forgive you. My boundary is not to see you anymore. Bye.

Haiku

You're not playing chess, you're on the board being played, a pawn wrapped in skin!

You're not playing chess,

you're on the board being played, a

pawn wrapped in skin!

Haiku

You envy and want
folk's victories but with that
their struggles come too.

You practiced hard to
be low hanging fruit and got
mad when you were picked.

If you won't think "outside of your box", you are living in a coffin.

You're being an accomplice to people who steal your time. Go reclaim that!

Stop overworking yourself for someone who considers you a job!

Haiku

You are allowing someone who can't do what you do, call you weak!

You are allowing

someone who can't do what

you do, call you weak!

Be for real! Stop asking people to treat you better than you treat you.

Ignorance is cheap. Knowledge is free. Stupidity is expensive!

Haiku

You call me the black sheep because I will no longer walk behind you.

You call me the black
sheep because I will no long-
er walk behind you.

Stop trying to impress them. You'll never be enough for the empty.

My haiku be battle
rapping with your
whole poem
so don't come for
me!

My haiku be bat-
tle rapping with your whole poem
so don't come for me!

Don't assume my inclusion in a group is my indorsement of them.

Haiku

You quote rappers but
you don't quote yourself. Puppets
don't always have strings.

Believe silence when
people do not answer you,
they did answer you.

If you don't post when
they get a F then don't post
when they get an A.

Haiku

Some of y'all are mad
at people who told you the
truth. Read that again.

Some of y'all are mad
at people who told you the
truth. Read that again.

Haiku

You can't do the right
thing with the wrong people and
get the right result.

You can't do the right
thing with the wrong people and
get the right result.

Haiku

> Iron sharpens iron
> but you don't want
> to get
> cut
> so you stay small.

Iron sharpens i-
ron but you don't want to get
cut so you stay small.

Stop congratulating ing folks you have no intention of supporting!

Haiku

> Some of you are trying to run your business the way your run your month.

Some of you are trying to run your business the way your run your month.

If someone tells you
get back in your lane, tell them
this is my highway.

Haiku

Come on now, my strength
is not debatable but
your loyalty is.

You are chasing "the bag" so hard, you left your integrity behind.

Haiku

You speak like you're playing spades. One firm truth, with "a possible" 2 lies.

You're the problem. You believed their lies. You didn't ask me if it was true.

Haiku

Your first strategy
should
be obedience.
Obedience to God.

Your first strategy should be obedience. Obedience to God.

Haiku

You married your regrets but you would not even date your potential.

You married your regrets but you would not even date your potential.

Haiku

You don't get to determine how someone expresses the pain that you caused.

Everyone who writes
is a weightlifter. Don't judge
a pen you can't lift!

Haiku

Underused words:
It was all my
fault. I was wrong.
I'm really sorry.

Haiku

> You believed their lie
> without checking
> with me, so
> they'll lie
> on you too.

You believed their lie without checking with me, so they'll lie on you too.

Your resistance to
logic is contagious but
I'm not getting sick!

Manipulation
is your favorite meal and
I won't eat with you!

In Your Face Haiku

Audacity is
on sale and you keep buying
it. Ain't you broke yet?

Haiku

Stop telling Blacks to deescalate something we did not escalate!

Being loyal to
someone with no loyalty
is stupidity!

Haiku

Let's speak truth.
Some of
you were a virus
before
Corona came out!

Let's speak truth. Some of you were a virus before Corona came out!

Haiku

I ain't doing the most. You're so used to small things, so I look massive.

Haiku

The shoe fits.
Are you
talking about me?
Yes,
Cin-der-lie-a,
I am.

The shoe fits. Are you talking about me? Yes, Cin-der-lie-a, I am.

Haiku

If information
I give you slides off
your tongue,
you ain't loyal son!

If information
I give you slides off your tongue,
you ain't loyal son!

Change what you do, not how you apologize. You gaslighting pyro!

You said truth is your
currency but your secrets
said that you are broke!

He is not that smooth
of a criminal. You're just
a bad detective.

Balancing your crap
is a full-time job and I
do not work for you!

Sometimes you are not
invited because
you're great
and they are just
good!

Sometimes you are not invited because you're great and they are just good!

Haiku

You're in or you're out
and if you're out your opin-
ion does not get in!

Stop talking about
cutting people off. You know
your knife ain't that sharp!

Haiku

Forgiveness is served with consequences. Grown up food isn't a kid's meal.

If someone says you
shine too bright, tell them to take
a seat in your shade.

Why is it the
job to
"stand on truth"
on those who
never said the lie?

Why is it the job
to "stand on truth" on those who
never said the lie?

Haiku

You can't teach me
how to row
a boat from the
shore.
You're a fake
expert!

You can't teach me how
to row a boat from the shore.
You're a fake expert!

> You "overbooked" yourself and got mad at the people you said yes to.

You "overbooked" yourself and got mad at the people you said yes to.

Haiku

You don't get to determine how someone expresses the pain, you caused!

Yes, they threw likes at
your post, but they don't like you.
Jealousy likes you!

You are wasting time,
proving you can do something.
For who? They don't care.

Haiku

When you're a walking
match, you're easy to gaslight.
You burn so quickly.

You can't bring flowers
to a funeral that
you caused.
Death keeps
receipts!

You can't bring flowers to a funeral that you caused. Death keeps receipts!

I'm a horror show
dressed as a love story but
you didn't read my script.

Haiku
Quieter Punch

If you're helping some
one, help them. Facebook doesn't need
to know that chapter.

Haiku

For "no" reason a monster attacked you. Maybe you're a monster too.

For "no" reason a monster attacked you. Maybe you're a monster too.

When did my pain turn
into background noise to a
life I did not script.

Haiku

You weren't there to make money. You were there to make sense. You made nonsense.

Why are you letting someone try to teach you something they've never done?

> If you'll settle for crumbs, why would they ever offer you a whole meal.

If you'll settle for crumbs, why would they ever offer you a whole meal.

> If you are not racing against yourself then you are on the wrong track.

If you are not racing against yourself then you are on the wrong track.

Haiku

Some of you do not
give out any flowers but
you want a garden.

Haiku

Mama, can you love me?
No sweetheart,
I don't know how.
Can you teach me?

Mama, can you love me? No sweetheart, I don't know how. Can you teach me?

Haiku

You're causing trauma,
but you have it wrapped up in
the word: honesty.

Haiku

When they congratulate you but they really mean...
How are you still here?

When they congratulate you but they really mean...
How are you still here?

Misery does not
love company but
misery
does knows
family!

Misery does not
love company but misery does knows family!

Haiku

If lions run with
lions and sheep run with sheep,
who do you run with?

Haiku

That is my past so
why do you keep
bringing it
up?
Old dirt, same you.

That is my past so
why do you keep bringing it
up? Old dirt, same you.

Stop letting media sound bites decide what you should chew on.
Go read!

Haiku

Math ain't hard.
Division can
multiply hate,
if you
add ignorance.

Math ain't hard. Division can multiply hate, if you add ignorance.

Some of you talk
about life because
you're "board" and
got no game,
talk less.

Some of you talk a-
bout life because you're "board"
and got no game, talk less.

If you don't believe
you have privilege that doesn't
mean you don't use it.

Don't add family
to your "to do list". They are
not your assignment.

As soon as you say
"no", you're the problem. Control
is the air some breathe.

They think you're a walking coupon because you keep discounting your worth!

Haiku

My tears screamed catch me,
but I was too busy
catching you.
Do tears cry?

My tears screamed catch me, but I was too busy catching you. Do tears cry?

Haiku
Whispering Facts

Haiku

Truth said: you are not keeping the peace, you are enabling a monster.

Will you feed me if
you don't know me or is
hunger personal?

Haiku

Does their hunger feed
your posting and likes
while your
inaction kills them?

Does their hunger feed
your posting and likes while your
inaction kills them?

Haiku

The day my smile died,
rain drowned my tears. No olive
branch could hold my pain.

Haiku

Their empty soul can't fill your empty heart. You can't skate on ice that thin.

Haiku

"Bee you" stop trying to be a mosquito. (No hate to mosquitos.)

Integrity is
a choice, just like persever-
ance is a lifestyle.

Haiku

> You have another excuse or another success. You can't have both!

You have another excuse or another success. You can't have both!

Racism isn't a
solution to pain. Don't bleed
on us, we didn't cut you.

Haiku

Each tear holds whispered pain. When a tear falls in the woods no one hears it.

The day my smile died,
rain drowned my tears. Love likes
me but pain smells so good.

True fact: if you listen to a lie long enough it becomes your truth.

I did not change my standards.
I changed my approach to get my standards.

Haiku

Rebound: stop asking someone who didn't break your heart, to hold it tighter.

Rebound: stop asking someone who didn't break your heart, to hold it tighter.

When you spill
someone's
tea, I wonder how
many
flavors did
your sip.

When you spill someone's tea, I wonder how many flavors did your sip.

Every assignment
you have is important. Don't
skimp on the free ones.

You're being distracted by the actions that you're meant to overlook.

Someone's moody
residue should not
find a home
in your inner
thoughts.

Someone's moody residue should not find a home in your inner thoughts.

Unaccompanied
minds can't make life decisions.
Shadows need the light.

Those people you thought
you needed did not miss the
boat. They chose to walk.

Haiku

You are green with envy but your bank account is still low, "cents" no change.

You are green with envy but your bank account is still low, "cents" no change.

Escape their neglect
and watch hope exhale slowly.
Peace whispers, you're safe.

Have you watched love dance
in the wind and disappear?
Passion said goodbye.

An apology
without change is gaslighting.
Show me how you changed.

Poet-factual Haiku

Memorization
is not poetry. Poetry is poetry!

Haiku

Just 'cause they don't poet, like you poet, that don't mean they ain't poets!

> Poetry heals, I
> don't think you
> heard me.
> This ain't no go
> game it's a cure.

Poetry heals, I don't think you heard me. This ain't no go game it's a cure.

**Stop letting people
who can't write try to define
you. Your blood isn't ink.**

Poets are not acc-
essories. Expose us to
cash not excuses.

Stop trying to write "non friction" poems and write your truth! Whispers don't scream.

Haiku

Dear poets,
don't let
another poet
decide
which ink
you bleed with.

Dear poets, don't let another poet decide which ink you bleed with.

My haiku be battle rapping with you whole poem. Pick on someone else!

My haiku be bat-
tle rapping with you whole poem.
Pick on someone else!

Haiku

You understand that
poets write about pain they
did not walk through. Right?

Haiku

Exposure nah! I'd rather be rested and broke than tired and broke.

Exposure nah! I'd rather be rested and broke than tired and broke.

Haiku

Understand,
only God can take
pen. Now
go
pick it back up.

Understand, on-
ly God can take pen. Now
go pick it back up.

Poet olympics
needs to stop, not the performers, just the judges.

Haiku

So, my pen does not
speak to you, that does not mean
my pen does not speak.

Haiku

One person's that
price is crazy
is
another
person's,
is that all.

One person's that price is crazy is another person's, is that all.

Procrastination:
you cliché yourself more than
you pursue your pen.

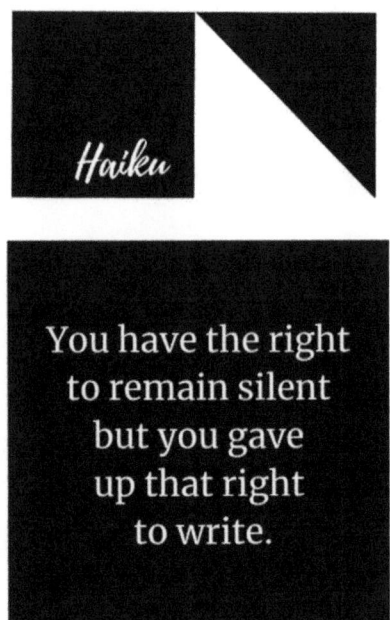

You have the right to
remain silent but you gave
up that right to write.

Don't let "them" talk you
out of doing something that
God told you to do.

Haiku

> Stop saying yes
> to things you
> don't want,
> for people
> you don't
> really need.

Stop saying yes to
things you don't want, for people
you don't really need.

We're sick of making
other people comforta-
ble, while we suffer.

Those who have never
tasted ink
don't know what it
is like
to miss it.

Those who have never tasted ink don't know what it is like to miss it.

How can you have mad
hate outside of the poem, you
can't even get in.

> If you have more knowledge now and you are not doing better than you used to.... then knowledge was never your problem. You are the problem!

Kimism (Kim's Saying):

If you have more knowledge now and you are **not** doing better than you used to…. then knowledge was never your problem. You are the problem!

www.ingramcontent.com/pod-product-compliance
Lightning Source LLC
LaVergne TN
LVHW061540070526
838199LV00077B/6853